About the Translator and Poet

Nader Rahimi is an Associate Professor at Boston University and has extensively published in the biomedical field. In recent years, he has developed an interest in poetry, and his first collection of poems, Songs of Being, published in 2021. Currently, he is working on his second collection of poems. Nader Rahimi lives with his family in the suburb of Boston, Massachusetts.

Siavash Kasrai was an influential twentieth-century Persian poet. His poetry had a significant influence on Persian literature, art, and music. Kasrai was the people's poet, and his poems championed the longing of the Iranian people for freedom. He was the Bertolt Brecht of modern Persia. Like Brecht's writings and poems, his poems are communicative art for a social cause. The scarlet stone is a tale of romance, sacrifice, betrayal, failure, and hope. The scarlet stone and other selected poems are the first-ever translation of Kasrai's poems into English.

The Scarlet Stone and Other Selected Poems

Nader Rahimi

The Scarlet Stone and Other Selected Poems

Olympia Publishers
London

www.olympiapublishers.com
OLYMPIA PAPERBACK EDITION

Copyright © Nader Rahimi 2024

The right of Nader Rahimi to be identified as author of
this work has been asserted in accordance with sections 77 and 78 of
the Copyright, Designs and Patents Act 1988.

All Rights Reserved

No reproduction, copy or transmission of this publication
may be made without written permission.
No paragraph of this publication may be reproduced,
copied or transmitted save with the written permission of the publisher,
or in accordance with the provisions
of the Copyright Act 1956 (as amended).

Any person who commits any unauthorized act in relation to
this publication may be liable to criminal
prosecution and civil claims for damage.

A CIP catalogue record for this title is
available from the British Library.

ISBN: 978-1-80439-588-2

This is a work of fiction.
Names, characters, places and incidents originate from the writer's
imagination. Any resemblance to actual persons, living or dead, is
purely coincidental.

First Published in 2024

Olympia Publishers
Tallis House
2 Tallis Street
London
EC4Y 0AB

Printed in Great Britain

Dedication

Dedicated to those who put their life and pens all for freedom.

Acknowledgments

I want to thank Bibi Kasrai for sharing the memory of her father with me and providing comments on the manuscript. I also want to thank Mojdeh Bahar, author and translator of multiple Persian poetry books, including *Song of the Ground Jay*, and *Milkvetch and Violets*, and Ida Rahimi for their valuable comments and edits to the manuscript.

Poetry outlives anything cast in bronze.
Roman poet, Quintus Horace

Translator's Preface:

Modern Persian poetry is intertwined with the aspiration of the Iranian people for freedom, their struggle toward an open society on the one side, and the brutality of repression and betrayal on the other side. Contemporary Persian poems often reflect a snapshot of this generational struggle and the failure of the struggle to bring about real political and social changes. Siavash Kasrai (February 25, 1927 – February 8, 1996) was at the forefront of this struggle, and poetry for him was a medium to use the rich tradition of Persian literature with mythological concepts and allegories to amplify the yearning of Iranian people for a free society. Kasrai's poems are inventive and progressive and champion the life of ordinary people who were struggling against repression and the apparatus of dictatorship in his native country of Iran. Siavash Kasrai was the Bertolt Brecht of modern Persia. Like Brecht's writings and poems, Kasrai's poems are communicative art for a social cause. His poems are mostly political, with a clear social dimension. These poems also put him in the crosshairs of both the former King Pahlavi (Shah) regime and the current ruling Islamic regime.

The publication of Kasrai's epic poem "Arash the Archer" (Arashe Kamangir) in 1959 gave him instant recognition among Iranian intellects and brought him fame. Arash the Archer is a work of unparalleled creative genius of modern

Persian poetry, which was woven into the remaking of the story of the legendary Persian hero, Arash the Archer, originally described by Ferdowsi in the Shahnameh (The Book of Kings) in the 10th century pre-Islamic Iran. Shahnameh is a literary masterpiece and cultural tapestry that remains to be one of the highest pillars of the contemporary Persian language and culture. The book of Arash the Archer by Kasrai is the voice of heroism in the face of defeat in an ominous time. However, it remained forever memorable with an unshaken endurance among the Iranians after its original publication nearly five decades ago. Arash is a legendary hero that saves his country from humiliation and defeat by putting his soul into an arrow, which travels over a long distance and ultimately determines the border between ancient Persia and Turan (tribes who were possibly living in modern central Asia and were in a constant fight with Persians) and gained back the lost territory. The scarlet stone (Mohreye sorkh)[1] is Kasrai's last publication. Although the Arash the Archer and the scarlet stone are stylistically similar (both are epic poems in a modern poetry style), their messages are deeply dissimilar, which reflects Kasrai's personal socio-political life experiences that witnessed the upending of the Shah's regime in 1979 and the political events that followed after. Arash the Archer is the primary protagonist of the story that symbolizes sacrifice, and salvation, which ends the humiliation and despair of his people, whereas the scarlet stone is a tale of loss, regret, blunder, rage, and yet a plea for understanding and reconciliation. Although in the Arash the Archer and the scarlet stone Kasrai is echoing the past, he argues for the present.

Sohrab is the love child of Rostam, a legendary Persian hero and one of the major characters of Shahnameh, and the main protagonist of the scarlet stone. The tale of the scarlet stone starts with the romance of Rostam with Tahmineh. The meeting of Rostam with Tahmineh begins in the city of Samangan (currently, a province in northern Afghanistan, which was part of Turan), when Rostam in search of his lost horse, Rakhsh, enters Samangan. When he arrives, the king of Samangan greets Rostam and offers him to stay for a night in his palace. That night, Tahmineh comes to Rostam's bedside and declares her love for him. Tahmineh believed that her union with Rostam would end the conflict between the two nations (Turan and Iran) and bring peace. Later that night, Rostam gives her a jewel from the band around his arm as originally told by Ferdowsi in the Shahnameh:

On the arm of Rostam, it was a scarlet stone,
It was famous around the world,
He gave it to Tahmineh,
If it is a girl,
Hang it on her hair
If it is a boy,
Place it on his arm,
A gift from father!

Shahnameh (The Book of Kings)

After that night and finding his stallion, Rostam returns to Iran. After nine months, Tahmineh gives birth to Sohrab. Years later, in a battle between Iran and Turan, after a bitter fight, Rostam tragically and unknowingly kills Sohrab.

However, when he discovers the jewel (the scarlet stone) on Sohrab's arm, Rostam realizes that he just killed his own son. Arash the Archer's action and his victory in war was an irenic victory (*i.e.*, was aimed at peace) that satisfied both sides and ended the war, whereas, in the scarlet stone story, Rostam's victory was a Pyrrhic victory that resulted in him killing his own son, Sohrab. However, Kasrai is more interested in exploring the shortcomings of Sohrab, a rising newcomer hero that brought this tragedy on himself rather than the Pyrrhic victory of Rostam. Sohrab is a proud and self-righteous hero and was ostentatious about it.

Arash the Archer and the scarlet stone in Kasrai's own words, "*Arash the Archer is the fruit of my youthful years, and the scarlet stone the legacy of my old age. If there are any similarities between them, it is just in style. However, each poem speaks about the events of their times that attempt to find an answer for the dashed hopes and disappointments. Although Arash and Sohrab are from the same bloodline, each bears different responsibilities. Arash jumps from the dam of death; he saves his life and the life of countless others. He is confident about his action and does not seek anything else. However, Sohrab is a young benevolent newcomer that has made an error and followed the wrong path. Armed with a sword, Sohrab is seeking justice but is unconvinced and fearful of the result of his action. At night, Sohrab sleeps with a smile and wakes up in the morning with fear and panic. Arash is thankful for his life and dies by his choosing. However, Sohrab is a spectator, fascinated with the seductive and glamor of life. He is naïve and brought misfortune to himself. In real life, people like Arash are few, but there are many like Sohrab.*

In the prelude verses of the Arash the Archer, Kasrai

champions the responsibility of humankind toward others. As if he anticipates the arrival of a new hero, like Arash the Archer, to save his country: Not from the foreign invasion, but the dictatorship of the Shah regime. The Arash the Archer is filled with literary and political symbolism that also concealed the true messages advocated by the poet. He dedicated the Arash the Archer to Khosro Roozbeh, a revered leftist activist and writer, who was executed by the Shah regime in early 1958. After his death, Khosro Roozbeh became the symbol of uncompromising resistance and opposition to the Shah regime.

Yes, yes, life is beautiful
Life is an everlasting temple of fire
If it is kindled, its dancing flames are seen from coast to coast
If it is dark, the darkness is our fault
Life needs blazing flames, and flames need firewood to blaze
Oh man, you are a forest!

The tale of the scarlet stone largely reflects the toll of the political development in Iran; his subsequent self-exile took on Kasrai's feelings, emotions, and more importantly his rearview mirror of the events that took place in Iran since then. In essence, the scarlet stone is an open letter of repudiation of the political ideology of the poet, in particular, and the political movement as a whole. The scarlet stone perhaps is more precisely a philosophical recognition of the failure, about the individuals who were wrong, took a wrong path, and the unfolded political events that followed the aftermath of the Iranian revolution in 1979. The scarlet stone is a fresh reinterpretation of this iconic Persian epic poem in the modern Persian poetry style. In this book, Kasrai through his unique lyrical and sharp investigative poetry style interrogates the history, the people, and confronts the intellectual and political blunders. In re-creating the story of the scarlet stone, Kasrai brings Ferdowsi (referred to Hakeem) to face Sohrab and listen to his grief (Hakeem is the creator of the hero, Sohrab). Here is Sohrab's conversation with Hakeem.

"With a drop of blood, you ended the story that at the start, love was writing a prologue,
You raised me so high,
Abandoned too soon!
When you were writing your book,
This wasn't your notion,
To every army corps, you gave a horse,
They happily lived a long life,
In the giant book of yours with a circle of a pen,
You made my father, that old hero, eternal!
You murdered a juvenile in the hands of this old hero!"

Hakeem initially struggles to respond to Sohrab's grief and complaints. He pauses and pleads for a time before responding to Sohrab. He tells Sohrab, "You were unprepared, unaware, and prideful, a young newcomer." Then he reminds Sohrab instead of railing at me or the enemy, you bear responsibility for this sad tragic incident. Here is Hakeem's response to Sohrab.

"When you willingly accepted to wear the scarlet stone on your arm,

You opened the door of tragedy on yourself.
You will find an answer for the cause of this accident in the scarlet stone."

In the scarlet stone, Kasrai shows the pungency of his mind in addressing the question of blind sacrifice in haste without full awareness (a rhetorical reference to individuals who fought for freedom after the Iranian revolution and lost their life). Although the tragedy of the death of Sohrab was not entirely in vain or wasted, it was avoidable. The tale of the scarlet stone is a brilliant manifesto for when our actions are not guided by responsibility and knowledge, which leads to tragedy and suffering. Even to the readers in Western societies, the tragedy of Sohrab's death is a powerful reminder that when our military and soft power apparatus are recklessly deployed against other nations, this often results in more plights and unintended consequences for others and us. However, despite the tragedy and death of Sohrab, Kasrai remains hopeful for a better world beyond the horizon.

"Sohrab, your blood
Among the red blood of Siavash, Esfandiyār, Rostam, and many other heroes
The knowns and unknowns,
Are spilled from all corners into the river of Shahnameh
This river will go on
Until it makes the barren plains green
From the memory of this soil, flowers will bloom."

This translation includes a complete translation of the scarlet stone, ten other selected poems, and a partially selected translation of the Arash the Archer.

The Scarlet Stone

Countless stories ended,
The old sorrowful crow has not yet arrived home,[2]
Still flying at the bottom of the eve,
Curiously listening to the stories from the beginning.

The heartbroken crimson night star
Dripping in the clouds,
the Simurgh[3] of the clouds
Is about to die in the nest of the night,
Wounded Sohrab[4] on the ground,
Burning and melting in the flames of fever.

If there was a sound,
It was the lonely neighing of an ill-faded horse
without a rider.

The music of footsteps was escaping from the desert,
The beginning of the end of an inevitable fate,
The rush of fever in his bloody bed pushed Sohrab to speak:
I am in flames, but I don't need water,
No, water will not remedy my thirst,
Hell to this thirst!
He shouted from his pain:
Damned mirage!

Mother, where is this place, Sohrab asked.
What am I up to?
Such dry clouds?
What a magical garden!

That old, that wise!
Who created these bitter fruits on the tree?
O mother who picked this bouquet, and from where?
Who unrolled this eternal feather bed for me?
Has everything in the garden gone with the wind?
What is left are all unripe fruits?

Rubies of blood,
Drips of garnet?
Who gave me this armlet?
Tell me, tell me, who left these roses at my bedside?

It is getting late, very late,
Father, hurry up!
Mother, tell me all about him and the excitement of meeting this hero,
Wipe away this fear from my heart!

Like a mother, the sky bent and kissed Sohrab's cheek.
Again, Sohrab looked around.

Tahmineh,[5]
In front of the mirror,
Drunk of Rostam's love,
She was humming and daydreaming,
The breath of the wind unfurled her hair.

The whisper of Rostam,
A lover from a distant land,
His footsteps on the palace doorway,
What forces led him to cross into the halls of my castle?
Was in the purse of the universe the hunting and loss of
Rakhsh[6] all an excuse to create a chance for me?

O' guidance of the universe!
On this special night, make my wish come true
You should hear my plea!
All the talking in this town,
Mountains and plains,
Buying and vending are about him
This palace,
This court,
All I have,
My heart and eyes are for him,
Now, he may arrive any moment.

O' mirror, tell me!
What shall I do, and how should I charm him?
What style should I do my hair?
Among all the colorful dresses, which one shall I wear?
How should I open up a conversation with him?
To draw his eyes' attention, what maquillage should I use?

Am I not important or alluring?
Who else other than Rostam could place dewdrops on the
flames of my flower?
Yes, who is worthy giving me the sole child of time?

A cloud moved in,
It looked like the cloud with a white cloth was washing away
fantasy from the weary eyes of Sohrab.
Mother, where am I?
Where is this horse with wings taking me?
Bridle in her hand, Tahmineh was sniffing the horse from
head to toe,
Touching the saddle, back, neck, and mane with inquest:

My only son, Tahmineh, said
Where did you go the fruit of my youth and love?
O' seed of the forest's hope?
What came about this tree with the branches of desire?
Why did you part from me?

I kept your name hidden,
Even Afrasiab[7] couldn't smell your secret scent,
Your vanity of good thoughts,
Your haste in meeting Rostam,
Blindfolded your wisdom.

With connivence, the enemy extended their hands to you
Yet, you were unaware!
It was a blunder to meet with the enemy,
You jockeyed on the horse in a stampede.

Tahmineh,
Head down on the saddle,
Pulling her hair and face,
Holding Sohrab's head in her arm,
Sobbing and whispering to herself.

How come at the end,
You concealed that famous scarlet stone on your arm,
under your garment
The only vestige from Rostam,
Without reason,
You made your unlucky father the most heartbroken and
infamous man in the world.

Sohrab was irritated and woeful,
He grinned then stopped talking,
He glanced again,
He was wearing the armlet, the gemstone of Rostam, in the
wrong place.

Then, he calmly said,
Mother,
I salute you and farewell,
It is a pity that death kidnapped your lap from me.

Mother!
Take this hidden scarlet stone off of me,
Without blame,
Give it back to Rostam,
The only man in the world who deserves it.
Stand up, wash your face off, and comb your hair
No more sorrow and grief.

Tahmineh,
While holding on to the bridle, softly picked up the saddle
and armor.

The horse was giving up in the darkness of the desert,
Briefly, she walks,
Head down and dragging her feet behind,
As if she was throwing flowers in the wind's way.

Farewell, my river,
My life,
My everything!
You were in vain!
A dead groom in the bridal chamber of the Shahnameh,
A groom without a bride,

My rosaceous cedar!
I thought of having a handsome and talented son
Would calm Rostam's zeal
And the companionship of father and son
Would burn down the roots of hatred
And spread wings of love on this land,

Now, my son,
My fleeting young deer
Fallen down on a hill on a foreign land,
Just now, your father,
Rostam,
That strong and unshaken mountain
In the mill of his sorrows,
Like a wounded stone,
Lonely, far from home, and cast down,
Here I am in the middle,
Like dust in a storm.

O' creator!
You gave me the best and took away my best,
What was this for?
What was this, and why?

Her shouting drew a line in the dark sky
She walked away,
Somber,
Blackened, darker than the night
The desert was sucking from the blackened leaves of the night
The plant of the night was growing taller from the soil of the desert,
A bird over the rock flow to the horizon.
The winds were carrying Sohrab's silent songs to faraway lands.

My dandelion flowers are all gone in the steam of the wind,
I knocked on many doors,
No heads peaked out,
No one offered me a candle.

Oh, it is getting late,
For the night traveler, there is no help other than the stars,
Carry no water with you,
O man of the wanderer!
Come back,
The fountains boil from your stone,
For a moment, sit down with me,
O your father's hero!

In pain,
Shedding tears,
Angry at himself,
Worn out and covered in dirt,
Rostam,
Standing at the side of a body without a heartbeat,
Touching his son's hair
A lion in the corner of a cage,
Like a waterfall, he is hitting his head on the rocks.

Of this shame,
The spinning of the universe arced,
This stain will remain in Rostam's heart forever
O' my river,
My hands are hurting
The eyes of my heart are turned blind,
My days are in darkness.

O' creator,
As you soared atop you crumbled my life.

They said,
A man has arrived,
A hero,
He is unrivaled in the world
No match for him other than Rostam
There will be no victory without Rostam.

Father and son, the two identical,
Being a stranger is a surprise,
With a hundred marks on your face and body

I didn't recognize you, and also you,
Who was this veil-holding magician and blinder?
How was I blindsided?

My heart had warned me:
Be cautious,
Breathe in,
Think twice,
It is a pity that my poor wisdom lured me,
Yea, he is an enemy!

Tearful Rostam bent over.
Putting his face on Sohrab's messy hair,
It seemed he was smelling a fallen flower on his soul.

For a long time,
In the path of truth,
I have been fighting for the people of this land,
I wasn't alone
Like my father,
Customary of our founding fathers,

The enemy out of luck faced us
You were unaccustomed and innocent,
You were being toyed with
Yes, although defeat in this war would be a shame,
This incident is regretful.

That damned wisdom of mine was lame,
The lips of my wisdom were sealed

From coast to coast, the roads were set for this ill-starred fate.
Rostam was sightless,
His name better be forgotten,
He welcomed the fight without searching for peace.

The enemy took away a piece of my heart,
Ripped my arm with deception,
What a dire reckoning they got,
Oh, I am such a fool
The door of my heart was fastened with thousands of locks of hatred with no keys
You had a deceitful blade in your hand,
Even the roads were warning me!
Finally, that blade landed in your heart.

Let's carry on. This is what the world is!
Our friendship and love were the envy of the enemy,
Our sorrow and distance brought joy to their misery.

As if Rostam was in search of a star in the clouds,
He gazed at the gloomy sky,
Still, he was not done speaking to his son:
Rostam lived a lonely life
Though he triumphantly overcame the seven labors[8] of Shahnameh,
Day after day, he was waiting for your union.

His eyes were in search of a handsome,
Young hero,
A son and a fighting partner.

Yes, life with hope is full of warmth,
It is ash without flames,
It is like the remains of the cold fire pit,
Now, Rostam is an ill-starred and ruined man.

Rostam was a hero,
A world champion,
Now, he is a broken man,
Joy to the travelers, who get home,
Lucky, who is calm on a fateful night?
The magical night brings them to sleep.

But for Rostam,
The unfinished road is ahead,
Good night!
The overflowing floodwaters can move the rocks.

Rostam was holding his son's hand,
With a sigh of regret on his lips
Weighted down by the darkness of his heart
Like a flying ghost, he was slipping into a well.

At night, he was like a woman rising from a pond of tar,
Sleeping in a parade
The sun was slumbering,
The moon's light was dim,
The evening was dark.

There were no sounds but echoes,
Sohrab was in pain

He was twisting himself,
Where is that surprise moonlight of the old tower?
Where is that bird? Where?
He turned to dust.
What happened to that resilient flower?
That unfamiliar scent, which was like a wet breeze,
All of a sudden, it blew on my burned and fervent soul.

Lost in midway.
Has anybody seen my deer in the wild?
Such white and soft flowers!
From the armor of the night, a cloud of dust appeared and crawled out.

Oh, my impatient dear Sohrab!
Midnight is past,
Morning is nearby.
You should go to sleep now!

Was our meeting more than this adventure?
Ultimate and fast,
Without regret, not worth watching,
A shooting star was passing beside another shooting star,
Or the dropping of a ball?

On this night, let me sink like a shadow
With all these feelings,
Shall I leave you alone?
With my love, I leave you with the lord!

No, Sohrab answered

Stay with me for a moment
In this short strait of our meeting,
at the height of the battle,
the enemy's hand robbed our wisdom
Our hearts opened the doors of love for each other
Our meeting was urgent for this event.
The love of a red meteor passed above us.

Strange feelings keep lovers away that way,
Yes, we haven't experienced love,
We found love like a bouquet in running water.

Now, we follow the path of the graveyard, and
die like lovers
But you!
My moving caress,
You are a passing wind over a feeble leaf,
Remember to place the riding of hurried love in all the robes and dresses.

Remember the time!
You are not eternal!
Be aware that this infinite is not infinite!
You can leave now,
Peace be with you!
Forever, you will live with me with love!

Dust was gathering with the breeze around the wounded bird
Cracks and holes were closing in on the night, and
The night was moving away like a ghost,

It was turning blind.

The sound of the wings of wonder
Occupied Sohrab's mind for a few moments and brought him back.
He opened his eyes and surveyed the dark ceiling of the sky,
He asked:
Is it real, or is it my imagination?
The doors of the sky opened like a flower, and
From the shadow of his bright heart a dark cloud.

Hakeem,[9] a man with a turban,
He was quiet,
Like bits of mist,
His hair frilled on his head and face,
The eagles were carrying his flying throne,
With each moment, it was getting closer
There was a notebook in his hand,
A flag of fire on his crown,
The birds began unrolling carpets for his arrival.

Dressed in a robe,
Thinking that his pain had lessened,
Sohrab stood up to greet Hakeem
With a shaggy face and hair,
His hand was on the dripping bloody wound,
He came forward like a broken man
Dragging and staggering,
He stood in front of the open Shahnameh, and
Greeted Hakeem.

O' great wise man and wordsmith!
With a drop of blood, you ended the story that at the start,
love was writing a prologue,
You raised me so high,
Abandoned too soon!
When you were writing your book, this wasn't your intent.

Oh, prince of justice
To every army corps, you gave a horse,
They happily lived a long life,
In the giant book of yours with the circle of a pen,
You made my father, that old hero, eternal!

What about me?
A fledgling man,
Yes!
You murdered a juvenile in the hands of this old hero!
This story tarnished Rostam's fame, and
left Tahmineh in crushing grief and sorrow.

Sohrab noticed a sad smile on Hakeem's face.
He paused and breathed again,
I was on the way here, innocent and curious.
With the hope of meeting a great hero,
I was like a drop of water heading toward the ocean.

Unaware,
There is a distance between man and his desire
No matter how hard one tries,
It is dangerous and deadly,
I headed on this road to build fairness and friendship,

Serve alongside my father,
Erase all hatred.

Disobey Kāvus and all who are demon minds
build a palace of friendship,
liberty and freedom shall be our ritual!
The doors of my palace will be open with goods and gold,
No one will go hungry on this land.

I thought, this war will be the end of all wars,
From now on, our world will be filled with love, peace, and blooming flowers,
Our signs and emblems will be on the quivers and arrows of warriors.

I had good intentions and believed in myself,
I had no fear of this journey,
I underestimated the enemy's intention, and
overlooked my mother's compassion and worries.

O' Hakeem!
How should I tell you?
Between the clouds, fog, and sky,
our guiding star was missing.
We were in a battle of death in the dark,
Father was fighting with his son,
The enemies with ugly faces lurked behind,
They were watching us.

Like the end of a burning candlelight
Sohrab was still rebellious and fiery,

Attempting to stand tall,

The mighty Sohrab continued his talk,
When I arrived there,
As if the world went upended,
Trickery was everywhere,
Friendships were concealed,
Father and son were killing each other with sword.

There was no one to intervene,
No one said a word!
No one extended a hand of friendship!

After years apart in waiting,
From behind the curtains of fog,
The shining eyes of my heart were not there to see the newcomer.

He was going to kill his son,
Or be killed!
Where was Zāl[10] and his wisdom?
Where was the guiding Simurgh?

Now my wound is like a Browallia flower spreading the scent of death,
Where is Kāvus Shah to bring medicine?

Those tight-lipped, silent people,
What kind of creator do they follow?
Who created them?
Are they all firewood helpers?

Sohrab,
Frantic as ever,
Touches his wound and sighs.

In his final hours,
With the gentleness of Rostam,
He was on the cold dirt,
Sleeping in the short-lived warmth of his mother's arms,
Like the short life of mist,
He was brimming with pain.

Life is good
When the misery of people
Like thorns of blame, don't tear open your heart, or
The colorful fruits and flowers of the tree of hope never
season.

In my country,
I was the bearer of no single history,
My fights, failures, loneliness, and sorrows were all a waste,
Cruel retribution for what sin?

Sohrab was frowning and silent,
leaning against his sword,
Tepid but inquisitive,
He turned his head toward Hakeem.

Hakeem was gazing hard at the dark curtain of the night,
Waiting in thought to reply,
As if the culprits of the plot were in his purview,
The ocean of fire, smoke, the stallion, darkness,

Blush of the blaze and horseback riding Siavash[11] were all in his sight.
Now, the fortress of Afrasiab,[12] the plain, the golden tub, and the blood,
The prince's head is tipped over.
Yet again, the troubles of Esfandiyār[13] and his destiny,
On the other side, the mischievous Shoghad[14] was trapped in the hunting field.

Rostam at the bottom of a well,
The final escape of King Yazdgered[15]
The miller[16] and Mahoyeh the Marzban[17]
That ominous war,
The surprise attack of the Arabs,
The tropical storm,
The whirlwind
The letter and rageful tears,
Of enlightenment for an ill-faded war,
The helpless man, Rostam Farghzad,[18]

The flames,
Like a headless chicken,
Were distressed,
Fluttering over the walls, the ceiling, and the doorways of the night.

Hakeem,
From the summit of his high place,
Was bent and observing Sohrab,
Maybe, he was searching for a chapter in his book
With pain and remorse,

Beyond any words,
He was about to speak.

Be at ease!
People envy your fame with chagrin,
You are Rostam's solitaire.
Take it easy now,
When you are on a perilous journey,
whining and grumbling are not helpful,
You are a strong hero,
In the tradition of heroes,
You should end this story.

Unread and unheard piles of pages of my writing,
Unacquainted with the turns and twists of the broken norms,
You enthusiastically put yourself in danger.
These words are unwarranted from you,
Why are you blaming me?
Who is running this country?
Where is the king?
Where is the army?

I aim to build this public palace[19]
Though it is a sorrowful verse,
I am a wise storyteller,
A mirror holder of conduct and bearer of time.

I am a gleaner of the farmer's harvest,
I retell stories and events as they happened,
And let history judge them.

However,
I wouldn't offer a loaf of bread,
without unhusking the kernels,
Until they pass the test of the mill of my hands,
Not without kneading the dough,
Not until it is backed under the flames of the oven of my thoughts.

But the tale of the death of someone dear like you,
You haven't known me behind the piles of these pages,
I wouldn't even order to harm a grain-carrying ant.[20]
No, I wouldn't kill!
People in different ways carry the heavy and silent wheels of their own death,
No, without reason, I wouldn't even pull a leaf from the branch of a tree in my garden.

The fire was spreading into the threads of the night's black mat,
Eager to hear the rest of his speech,
Sohrab hurried.

When you willingly accepted to wear the scarlet stone on your arm,
You opened the door of tragedy on yourself.
You will find an answer to the cause of this misfortune in the scarlet stone.
Sohrab, that jewelry on your arm,
That armlet, yes!
It is the armlet of the worldly hero!
Whoever wears it is a hero behind the borders of his own

country.

You were unprepared,
You were unaware and buoyant.
A young newcomer,
Even before opening your eyes,
A stranger gave you such a priceless armlet!
Yes, that armlet, that gemstone,
that ruby you wear on your arm,
like the seeds of a charming magician,
thrown on the fire,
it takes you away from home,
it makes you homeless.

Yes, with the blink of an eye
It connects you to a city, to a place, and with many people,
Unfamiliar with their love and hate.

But with the passage of nights and days, months, and years,
The seeds of time,
Quietly chow and tear up the brocade of life and delight.
That armlet brings upon you all the evilness and baseness,
Poverty and ignorance,
Tyranny and fear.

Like an inscription,
The world's pain is visible in front of your eyes.
It wakes you up,
It makes you rise, and
fight with the camp of injustice until your last drop of blood.

Although your heart was to serve your country,
The world was lined up an army to face you,
You were the target of every fatal arrow.

In fencing, you hurt or get hurt!
It can cause you pain and injury,
But it is more hellish than death,
When the universe wants to defeat the hero of a book,
Or frustrates him to give up,
Then,
A massive task is not just about self-trust and virtuous thoughts,
In the halls of the darkness of ignorance, happy are those who find a light of wisdom in their own sorrow.

Still, the armlet had a mark,
It had the color of Rostam's envy and fearsomeness,
It grew wings from Tahmineh's swift and restive love, and
Flew your wishes to high places.
So, be quiet!
Don't unjustly accuse anyone else,
The armlet was not displayed in the right place,
It dragged your wounded body into the waves of my verse.

At the end of the plain,
The night's tent was about to be removed,
or the wall of the day was raising on the horizon,
The night was fleeing.

But Hakeem still had words to say:
I am ashamed of those who turned their back on their

country and people
With hundreds of excuses, they allied with the enemy.
It doesn't get any better. What can you do, and nothing to say about them?
Why do they start turbulence in this land?
Happy are those who wholeheartedly serve without malice,
Winning or losing is out of our dialog,
Happy are those who have chosen the right path.

When you are walking on the seashore,
You are away from the deadly currents of the ocean,
But without diving deep,
One gets no pearls from the seashells.

Sohrab,
O' wounded of ignorance of darkness,
There is medicine in the corner of King Kay Kāvus palace,
But it's not good for your wound.
Yes, you are not thirsty for water; water is under your feet.

Hear me, Sohrab,
Enlightenment is the remedy for your wounds,
The rocky river of wisdom is your place.
Let me tell you a secret about the armlet.
This glorious armlet can bring you a blessing or curse,
It is a panacea of eternity and death,
It is a poison, a drink of poison in a glass of ruby,
Only lovers drink this wine,
It can suddenly kill,
Like the killing of dawn by the rising sun.

Now, is it time to get help from the selfish King Kay Kāvus?
You were always a clear danger to him,
Or from Zāl, who is unaware of your fight,
He could burn Simurgh's feather to heal your wounds.

It's vain to complain about this and that,
The end of the inevitable is upon you,
Take a closer look at yourself,
Your bitter end was unavoidable.

O' dear hero!
O' eternal young man,
You travel around and show your wounds to anyone who carries a sword,
Show your wounds to the tired and anxious heroes who are uninformed about wheels and deals.
From now on, lovers will not follow the wrong path,
With scarlet light, they will follow the right track.

Sohrab, your blood
Among the red blood of Siavash, Esfandiyār, Rostam, and many other heroes,
The knowns and unknowns,
Are spilled from all corners into the river of Shahnameh,
This roaring sea will run away from the churlish loop of time.

This river will go on
Until it makes the barren plains green,
This is blood, boiling blood,
From the memory of this soil, flowers will bloom,

If the wisdom's mighty and holy hand,
could bring a scent of the memory to the present,
The visage of wish wouldn't be looking grim and discontent
at the ceiling.

At sunrise, at the far end of the plain,
A wave of light was touching the dark skyline,
Hakeem was pondering and whispering,
I fought for this book,
Not with a sword,
But with my pen,
Every word was a sprint for my life,
A lifetime's work,
I covered the events of the time with foresight.

My bitter goodbye to Rostam,
He is at the bottom of a well,
The end of tyranny and conquering,
Goodbye to thousands of fables,
The end of an inevitability.
A prologue to the open book of time.

After a short pause,
Hakeem turns to Sohrab and starts talking again.
Look at the moving sea from the window of the horizon,
The eternal lost ship carrying the entrusted armlets is sailing.
For better or worse, it's on the ocean now,

This beautiful and exquisite cradle is yours,
Your history, tragedy, anthem, and letters of cruelty,
The golden letters of wisdom,

Your thirst for justice,
The scent of love,
The king letters of yours,
The letters of your lineage.

I hope, at the safe shores,
People welcome it,
The enlightened people will build a harbor for it,
It will dock and unload there.

Sohrab was brimming with joy and happiness.
Holding the armlet tightly in his hand,
He staggers to his feet,
Quietly sits,
Then falls asleep.

Across the book,
Like a light shadow,
A swan on the water,
But Hakeem
Teardrops on his face,
Slowly, like holding a sleeping baby in his arms,
Closes his torn-apart book,
Sowing from his eyes scarlet dew on the leaves.

In the eyesight of midday,
A horse walks away with head and tail down,
Without a bridle,
The scarlet-colored sun,
Like an armlet was sitting on the arm of the sky.

Arash the Archer[21]

Snowfall,
Snow falls on the thorn bushes and rocks,
The mountains were silent,
Valleys were tense,
The roads were waiting for the caravans with the sound of bells,
If smoke was not rising from the chimneys on the rooftops of huts,
If the lantern's flickering light was not a hint,
If our footprints did not mark the icy roads,
What would we do in this snowstorm with its frightening thunder?

I'd told, life is beautiful
To say or not to say, the point is here
The open sky,
The gardens of flowers,
The golden sunlight,
Wide and horizonless plains,
The sprouting of flowers from underneath snow
The soft dance of fish in the crystalline water
The smell of rain-soaked soil in the mountain
The sleep of wheat fields under the moonlight.

Coming, going, running,

To love,
To feel the sorrow of man,
To stump in people's happiness,
To work, to work,
To relax,
To see the scenery of the dry and thirsty desert,
To sip fresh water from a newly filled jar
To run the sheep to the pasture in the early morning,
To singalong with birds of the mountain,
To feed the trapped baby deer and set them free,
To rest in the valley in the midafternoon…

Yes, yes, life is beautiful
Life is an everlasting temple of fire,
If it is kindled, its dancing flames are seen from coast to coast,
If it is dark, the darkness is our fault.

Life needs blazing flames, and flames need firewood to blaze,
O' man, you are a forest!
The streams flow over your shadow,
The sun shines, the wind blows, and the raindrops fall upon you,
The nests on your fingertips forever rest,
You are a noble servant of the garden of fire,
O' forest of man, be proud and stay forever green,

Once there was a time,
A dark and bitter time,
Our fate, like the face of our enemies, was dark,

The enemies were overriding our life,
Life was as dark and cold as a rock,
On the day of infamy,
A shameful time…
There were fears and death's wings.
Nobody was moving, not even a leaf on the tree branch,
The trench of freedom-lovers was silent,
The enemy's camp was jubilant.

There was no love in people's hearts,
No one was helping one another,
No one was smiling.
The garden of hope was leafless,
The sky of tears was full of rain.

I'm Arash, the freedom army,
The man of work and grief,
Mysterious, like a meteor from the night,
Like a ready-morning visit…
However, today's preparation is not about clout and championship,
In this fight,
On this fateful and unwavering arrow,
A feather should be taken of the being, not letting it stop flying…

Roots and Forest

I am a branch of the pine forest,
Don't remind me about getting hurt,
From the strikes of an ax on my trunk,
I have unforgettable memories,
Not once, was being hurt, not a surprise.
Spring brings more memorable surprises.
If a hundred times, they bring me down,
If a hundred times, they break my bones,
From my firewood, flames will rise,
From my roots a forest.

Wish

Like a rift of soil flowering in springtime,
Rushing toward the glowing particles of the sun's radiance,
To become a wave on the seashores of a vast ocean,
Finding endless get-up-and-go in a long journey.

O' eye of the sun,
My heart is yours; it is following you,
On this spring morning,
O' flower, be happy sprouting is yours,
Ah, time, my feet are moving slowly, my hands are getting weak,
My spring nightingales are silent.

It is a cold occasion,
And the cold occasion is held with iron claws,
and is placed in the warm houses of hearts and souls,
That withering lamp,
This cheerless land,
I am stricken with a cold,
I am hardening like a stone,
My heat burner heart is frosting,
I am becoming lonesome,
This broken heart is becoming desolate again,
I have a pious asking,
I am turning into stone and still, this patient stone is a

prisoner of fire.

Dear friend, it's a pity that our hope is gone,
From that booming fire, all that is left is smoke,
Whatever happened, it is behind now,
It was a brocade of a wish that is now without sinew and bone.

My roaring voice is becoming silent,
The memory of the time is forgetting my grief, joy, love, and hope,
Once, there was a spring inside me, a colorful flower,
A bird,
The calmness of the valley,
The roaring of the moving river,
Rain giving clouds,

There was a blossom inside me,
A sprout,
A timeless desire,
Thousands of jewels of night cries,
Now, the flowers of the garden of my heart are slowly withering and losing colors one after another,
The rumpus of my thoughts is becoming quiet,
All I had had turned to stone,
You and the memory of your face will turn to stone with me,
You will turn to dirt with me,
Yes, at the end of the night, I will turn into a stone,
With fire in my heart,
A melody on my lips.

Like a glowing particle,
The soil,
A wave,
A plant.

Desert Nights

Desert nights are free of all bonds,
The silent desert nights are the silence of the winds,
In public or private,
The desert thorn opens its arms in the middle of the desert,
Its stern bush, like an old warrior, sings a singalong with the wind.

O' infinity,
I'm that plant with the hope of living,
Have roots everywhere in the soil,
O' infinity, even one flower hasn't flourished from the hands of mine, thorns,
I've flourished a flower with reed everywhere,

Yes, it's me who is burning in a thirst for water,
Rivers are all shy from this perilous desert,
I'm waiting for a cloud and rain, but alas!
If a cloud reaches me, it's like a passing horse,
I am tearful from the rainless sky of this desert,
Where have the dark and the clouds with the rain gone?
I am nothing more than a silhouette.
Where are the wild sandstorms of the desert?

If this rope wasn't tied to my foot,
I would have run away someday like a dove,

If I weren't interested in this soil,
I would tear my robe like the wind on my body one night,
O' those who are out of my eyesight,
O' forthright road,
O' those who are gone far beyond my circle,
O' unruly wind,
I have a word for you,
A single word, a single message,
The desert nights are free of all bonds,
The silent desert nights are the silence of the winds.

To the Redness of Fire, to the Flavor of Smoke

O' the name of joyous freedom!
With many blunders,
With many failures of ours,
Will I see your birthday in my lifetime?
Will you bloom O hidden flower?
Will you sit in on my poem one day?
Will you grow together with my kids?
O dormant seed,
Will your tree give shade in our desert one day?

I told myself to worry no more,
It's a pity that my heart is taken by the sweetheart of sadness,
Yell, O' friends yell!
Dying from my slim patience,
I am mournful,
When pride pulls its eyes with its own hands,
And hatred marks a furrow in the futile lands,
When the runaway deer,
Sick of touring the slaughterhouse of love,
Eager for freedom in the plains with no boundaries,
Every moment,
In the passage of curfew,

They expose their noble hearts to the target.

I am saddened,
I am taken by the sadness,
On my eyes,
Grief marks the land and the moment dark and ruined.
Whether a hand, again,
From the supreme height of the forest,
From the narrow valleys,
From the secret chest of spring,
From the parched heart of rocks and sands,
Will pick from the bloody thorn bushes?
Whether even now,
The sole fruit of freedom,
That first fruit,
Should be found inside the green basket,
That is all?

In the wailing wind,
There is a woman that bears out,
At the foot of the cradle of these mountains and hills,
A sorrowful woman who sings a lullaby.
O' my darling wildflower,
O' golden poppy blossom,
O' the fifteen[22] blessed bloody feathers,
These young stems were windswept from their heads.

You will live in the garden of my memory,
I will plant the essence of your hopes in the chambers of my heart,
On the eve of the New Year, without a name, I will carve on

the old tree of Esfand
Your auspicious name, O' crashed Siahkal.

I said they don't kill anybody with firing squads,
I said the blue color of martyrs is a lover.
I am unaware, my friend.
Far away from your sorrowful gaze, it's of my foul mouth.
They detain without notice,
They murder without a name,
They silence the sound of the anthem and Sirius.
With cunning and deception,
They veil the newly grown rosy flowers
Against our desire,
A flower to the redness of fire, to the flavor of smoke.

Oh, Rose Blossom

Oh, the wind swept away the rose blossom
The rose heart stiffened from the pain
The nightingale said before leaving the orchid
My spring is over
My singing is done.

Song

I am a cloud coming over from the ocean
Going around from field to field
Show me the thirsty fields
I am a rain-full cloud.

A fugitive Swallow from spring
A guest on this field for a night
Came from behind the crops like a moon
Come visit me, waiting to see you!

In the dream, we were near the fountain
With one glass, you took away the moon from the water,
Once we sipped from that hearty glass,
You became a water lily, and I turned into a moonlight tear.

You asked me to take a leap in the dark and make the ocean ours,
My heart turned into the ocean,
I gave my heart to you,
Care for it, don't let the ocean get bloody.

The light from the rooftop was my wrap at night,
A blue flower in my wheat field,
If it shines today with others,
Then one day people will know she was my sweetheart.

You and I stem from the same root
A new plant of the same root,
What does separation bring to us?
Slain by a sword from the root.

In the dawn of morning, in the narrow valley
The hunters ambushed
The lonely deer in the valley
Rubbing their piercing heart on the rocks.

O' deer with fire wings,
With a golden horseshoe and a silk mane
You left this saddened land, and I see nothing behind but dust.

The forest is covered in moonlight tonight,
The tiger of the mountain is asleep tonight,
On every branch of the tree, a heart has settled,
My heart is impatient tonight,

It is nightfall; the walk is long, and the time is short
The sky and the land are colored ruby-red
The desert is drunk from the sound of the caravan's bell
My dear, there is no time to waste.

My heart is the garden of martyrs
From the lives of tulips, my heart is rending
Friends, there is no road to the hamlet
My heart is a desert within the desert,

It is far away from one country to another
It is too far from here to my sweetheart's home
Finding time to visit friends
It is too far away to meet friends.

Don't braid your tangled hair
O nervous river wash away your sorrows,
Fill up your body with the sun's rays
The night will stir your turns and twists.

A flower takes root at the bank of the river
An alien follower in pig-tails
It is springtime, and I am not accustomed to the desert full of followers.

Daylight is rising
In my woeful heart, I am a sorrowful man
If you are a cradle, night – you open up the daylight
Where should I sleep to see you in my dream?

The road is not visible, there is no tour guide
Nor is there a glimmer of friendly light
I should run away from the trap of this night
I have no horse to ride or feet to walk.

Why is this garden treated with such cruelty?
Why are the spring songs forgotten?
Why are the nightingales silent?
Why is the hope of being a follower lost?

There is a latent fire in the ashes

There are many unspoken words on my lips
I am a silent coast with a heavy heart
A storm in my throat.

Your gaze was my sky, which I lost
Your eyes were my shade that is gone
Under the sky and upon your shade
The world was beneath my sight, which went missing.

To whom can I share the grief of the ocean-hearted man?
Where should I look for an ocean-hearted worrier?
My heart is an ocean of blood from the grief of a friend
How can I give up this ocean?

The plain-picked basket of flowers
The dawn of spring, plains, hiking, the breeze, and the scent
of green flowers are good luck charms.
They brought the message to town and left.

I am a breeze, a roadrunner with no return,
Covered in the dust – this is my story
I am brimful of memories of odors and colors of flowers,
I am missing the mountain and plains
I feel like autumn
Worried more than ever
I am lonely in the city of lovers
A stranger in my town.

Happy to the stirring flight of the spring?
Among the runaway clouds
Mountains are void of the echoes of laughter,

It is a pity for the Quails of the mountain.

My spring blossoms at your look,
In loving you, my heart turned into a garden of flowers
Swallows of your black eyes
Nested on the rooftop of my dreams.

Make a road with a flame in my flesh
Put your blushed tongue on my dress
Throw me on the fire and turn me into ashes
Turn me into a light in the darkness.

I am a harp lying down in my sorrows
Silence at my lips, turmoil in my heart
Lonely inside, joy and music in my thoughts
With broken bones, a tune in my mind.

Poppy flowers are dead near the rocks,
The water is frozen,
Larks have left the mountains in the dark,
Spring has arrived, dressed in green,
A flower on her hat, a rose-bush on her belt,
I am a frost with no more tears,
What shall I do if she comes to my home?

The camp is shrouded in mist,
The land and sky are mourning,
What kind of season does this that freezes the heart?
What kind of city is this where its land is in sorrow?

I washed in the fountain,

Stayed on the rocks and dirt.
Fresh air was in my mind.
It's a pity that I became acquainted with dirt.

In the dawn of morning's sounds and embrace, which fill up this golden-dressed desert
Flowers are sitting in the desert's lap,
With my silent lips, I ask you to be my spring.

You are lonely without me; I am all alone without you,
There are miles and miles between us
The wheels of life made a distance between friends,
The mark of this shame is on the sun.

The joyous Larks flew away.
They gave up on our land,
Left behind this cold land,
They are on their way to sunny cities.

My black-eyed spring flower,
To see your hands around my neck,
I circle around you,
I am a bird who jumped from your rooftop,
Not knowing I am chained to your feet.

Mountain, I wish you good health,
That your furnace stays forever warm and your water cold.
Never tumble into the hands of cowards
Your deer stay awake, and your friends remain brave.

Two deer passed from this desert,

They left quietly without fear,
From this barren land,
They left together but lonely.

Man's Home

Sky is the nest of fantasy birds,

The planet is man's home.

Sky is vast
but empty,

The planet is small
but full.

Gypsy Girl

A wild twister is my love
A girl of the desert and frenzy of the mountain
A restless gypsy girl is my love
Joyous, wanderer and a walker
The desert wind is her companion.

She ignites a fire at night and falls asleep, jaded on the coast
The fire advances on the ocean, and the blue waves push the flames away
She is asleep on the soft sands.

At daytime, she is on the misty roads
Hiking in the heart of the green forest
At nighttime, she offers the night before the stars
And soars like a cheerful butterfly.

A restless gypsy girl is my love
Her visits know no borders
She is winced by people,
Darling and pretty
She is estranged from the city.

If she stuck in the sinkhole of love,
Her sweet water turns bitter
Like a calm overflowing river

She seeks a new bed at every moment
She is unacquainted with the blocks and alleys of the city.

The day will come,
She will come and give me a hug
She will walk on my land
One day that barefooted wild
Will slow down and touch me
The winds carried the news.

One day, my love, the gypsy girl will come
She will twist herself all over me,
Like the old forest hair,
Like an old sycamore tree, she will shin up around me
The gypsy girl will nest on me.

I will flourish in her arms
Get drunk from the odor of her body
Drunk from a thorn bush, a thornbush of the desert
Drunk from the unclipped beauty
I will nest nearby a snake.

Snake's eyes remember many tales
From the sunset that plunges into the ocean
The secrets of the raining mist in the wetland
A fire pit that was left behind in the desert
Fables of the golden rivers.

Tales of past cities
The land of sun and swallows
The suffering of people of faraway lands behind the blue

mountains
Wide agonies of the roads.

Colors of the followers he has smelled
The names of girls whom he has kissed
The beauty of colors
He dances at the parties of the desert people.

My love, love of a stray gypsy girl
She has a black talisman made from the roots of trees around her neck
Rain is her gift
The dawn of morning is a time of love and wandering.

I am the sin of a bitter drunken night
She is a wild plant in the desert
In gypsy love
We are both lost on the endless road
As a sign of friendship, we planted a thorn bush.

In the early morning, a mixed strain will flourish on the ice of someone's heart
A flower will sting nature
From sin, a drip of stars and a tear of love will fall on the clean plains.

She will no longer stay with me
She doesn't want to see me sulk,
I don't want to see her too.
She moves out with the shade of the clouds
Toward an unknown city.

Once the rain starts to fall on the forest,
When the birds begin singing in the wasteland, in a sunset, behind the cane field,
My eyes will run to greet her.

On this brown colored road,
Inside the mystery-raising mists,
The moaning of the wheels inside the fountain,
The moaning of wheels of the gypsy girl's chariot.
Like the melodies of a broken heart.

The pulse of melodies of the chariot's wheels surge throughout the universe
The sound of my heart is the pulse of wheels inside the fountain
Banging music in my chest
It's the sound of her chariot's wheels.

One day she will come and remove the grime from all over this land
And the pale look of the land will gain life again
She will emerge out of the dream and begin walking.

In my palm, I have a black talisman
A souvenir from a day of rain
Made from the root of a wild tree, and
The seeds of bitter love and lost
I like my black talisman.

Believe

My heart doesn't believe in his death
No, I don't accept this truth
As long as I am in the fellowship of the breath of life,
I wouldn't think of death
That being said, how could a flower be turned into dirt?

I have countless appointments,
Many travel plans,
My hands have yet to carry on with many prays
What will happen to these?

Above all, how is it possible for this many lovers
Afar from home,
On their path, one day, they will be silenced without a sound.

Should I believe that young girls with a bright future,
Alone and hopeless
Standing on the roofs and the front doors
Will dress in black waiting for their loved ones?

I doubt love can be held in a grave,
Rebellious flowers couldn't be kept from rising off the ground,
Should I believe my heart will stop beating one day?

Curse this lie, a fearful lie.

My poems will make a bridge to the coast of the future
The followers of joy will march on it
From their kisses and hands, my message will fly
Let the lovers see the peace carrier's path.

With man's achievement
The name of the man becomes eternal in the memorial tablet of time.

Without doubt,
Bit by bit, the warmth of our silence,
Will strike one day somewhere and turn into the sun.

If we love each other,
From our love, tears will roll down our cheeks
Till there is one live lover,
Death will never erase my name from the memory of time.

I have lost a bundle of flowers to the wind,
But sorrowful me,
The petals of the memory of no one would die with me,
The loss of no loved one is believable.

Finally, my leaves will fall one day
One day my eyes will fall asleep
No one escapes from this sleep
But the scent of my belief will fill the air of the garden.

The Enchanter Serpent

Take off these chandeliers from the ceiling,
Overthrow the light so that it dies,
Take the eye-harming smoke away,
Pull down the flame so that it wouldn't survive,
Take away the glass, take away the wine,
Leave the wine in the glass kisses
Keep the rave free from the fanfare,
Take slow steps, walk silently,
Tell the gatekeepers to keep the gates shut,
Tell the night travelers to stop singing,
Ask the guards to stay put,
Ask the night guards not to ride the horses,
Talk quietly, the enchanter serpent is sleeping…
Cover, cover that aperture!
Make the dark night darker.
It hasn't been a long time since the enchanter serpent has been sleeping,
Leave them all and pass this night!

End Notes:

[1] Mohreh in Farsi can mean a stone, or an armband (a bracelet worn high on the arm, rather than on the wrist). In ancient Persia, the great heroes used to wear armbands that signified their loyalty, and stature, which dates back to the Archimedean dynasty. In Shahnameh, Rostam was referred to as "Jahan Pahlavan" a brave and world-class hero, a title of honor granted by the King. Even in today's modern Iran, the most celebrated and world-class wrestlers wear an armband that signifies their world-class status. In addition, Mohreh in Farsi can mean an agent or a member (e.g., a government agent). In the author's view, the translation of Mohreye sorkh to "the scarlet stone" best describes the essence of Kasai's poem.

[2] Derived from the Persian idiom "Our story ended; the crow has not made home".

[3] Simurgh is a mythical bird in Persian mythology. It is likened to other mythological birds such as a phoenix. According to Shahnameh (book of Kings) of Ferdowsi, Zāl, the son of king Saam, was born albino. Samm thought his son Zāl was the offspring of devils and abandoned the infant on the Alborz Mountain. Zāl's cries were heard by Simurgh, who lived atop the Alborz Mountain, and she recovered the infant and raised him as her own.

[4] According to Shahnameh, Sohrab is the son of Rostam.

[5] According to Shahnameh, Tahmineh is the mother of Sohrab.

[6] Rakhsh, is the stallion of Rostam as described by Ferdowsi in the Shahnameh.

[7] Afrasiab was the mystical king and hero of Turan and also an arch-enemy of Iran as described in the Shahnameh. According to Persian mythology, he was an agent of Ahriman (God of evil and darkness), who was gifted with magical powers of deception to destroy Persian civilization.

[8] A series of difficult and dangerous acts were carried out by Rostam as told by Ferdowsi in the Shahnameh. Similar to the labors of Hercules, an ancient Greek hero.

[9] Hakeem, is the title of Ferdowsi. In Farsi, it means wise man/philosopher/thinker.

[10] Zāl, is a mythical Iranian king and is one of the greatest warriors of the Shahnameh. He is the father of Rostam.

[11] Siavash was a legendary Persian prince and son of King Kay Kāvus. His horse's name was Shabrang Behzād. In Farsi, it means night-colored purebred. His name in Persian literature is a symbol of innocence.

[12] According to the Shahnameh, Afrasiab is the name of the mythical king and hero of Turan, the archenemy of Persia. He was described as an agent of Ahriman (evil), who was gifted with magical powers of deception to destroy Persian civilization.

[13] According to the Shahnameh, Esfandiyār is a legendary Persian hero, the son, and the crown prince of the Kayanian King Goshtasp and the grandchild of Kay Lohrasp. He is best known for his tragic battle with Rostam.

[14] According to the Shahnameh, Shoghad was the half-brother of Rostam. He has always been jealous of Rostam's high status. He ultimately killed Rostam by dropping him into a pit full of swords and poisoned spears at the bottom of the well.

[15] Yazdgered was the last king of Sasanian dynasty of Iran from 632 to 651 AD. He was unable to repeal the Muslim Arab invasion of Iran. He was fleeing from one province to another with hope that he could muster enough army to fight the Arbs invasion.

[16] Yazdgered was killed at the hands of a miller near Marw city. Marw was a major Iranian city, which is located near today's Turkmenistan.

[17] Mahoyeh the Marzban, a border guard, was also involved in the plot to kill king Yazdgered.

[18] Rostam Farghzad was a military marshal during the reign of Yazdgered. He was appointed by Yazdgered to defend the empire. He is remembered as a historical figure and an important character in the Shahnameh.

[19] a reference to Shahnameh

[20] Perhaps, it is a reference to Persian poet, Saadi's well-known poem: Do not harm a grain-carrying ant, it is live and has a joyous life.

[21] A partial translation

[22] Esfand, the twelfth month of the Iranian calendar, when fifteen people were killed on February 8, 1971, by the dictatorial regime of Shah (Pahlavi regime) in a fire squad style in the failed uprising known as the Siahkal movement. Siahkal is a town in Gilan province. The Siahkal movement marked the beginning of the guerrilla arm struggle against the Pahlavi regime that ultimately led to Iranian Revolution in 1979. The Siahkal movement had a major impact on Iranian literature, poetry, and movies.